BRANDING

CONCIERGE

MEDICINE

By Michael Tetreault

Romans 15:13

I pray that God, who gives hope, will bless you with complete happiness and peace because of your faith. And may the power of the Holy Spirit fill you with hope.

Contemporary English Version (CEV)

BRANDING

CONCIERGE

MEDICINE

**The Blueprint That Shows You How To Apply
The Foundational Principles of Effective
Marketing
To Grow Your Medical Practice.**

Author: Michael Tetreault

Publisher Elite MD, Inc.
4080 McGinnis Ferry Road
Building 800, Suite 801
Alpharetta, Georgia 30005

"Michael is probably the foremost source of information in the world on concierge medicine and he has, through content research and engagement with the concierge care community, built Concierge Medicine Today into the most recognized and respected source of information for direct care medical professionals. He is very well versed in healthcare issues.

Beyond that, Michael is an expert marketing strategist for healthcare businesses and nonprofits who is excellent in the areas of brand development, messaging and push strategies. His knowledge of current and emerging social media platforms is extensive."

DEANNA BAXAM
Attorney
Baxam Law Group

"Michael freely provided direction and much needed assistance when I left my job to open up a solo concierge practice. He encouraged me to remain independent and build a practice as unique as I am. In so doing, I am 16 months in and will never look back."

SARAH MILDRED GAMBLE, DO
Signature Concierge Physicians & The Medical Offices of Sarah Mildred Gamble, DO

"Michael has one of the most creative brains I've run across in my 30+ years in business! He is thoughtful and brings not only creativity but a solid research and business acumen to the table."

ROBIN RAILEY ALTLAND
Executive Director
Marketplace Alliance Group

Publisher Elite MD, Inc.
4080 McGinnis Ferry Road
Building 800, Suite 801
Alpharetta, Georgia 30005

TABLE of CONTENTS

Dedicated to …

My Savior, Jesus, the God of Heaven and Earth,
the center of my life …

Catherine who saw the best in me years ago …
and continues to guide, lead and believe in worthy causes …

Kelly who continues to help me be my best every day …

INTRODUCTION

By Michael Tetreault

Concierge Medicine has always had somewhat of a "brand/identity" problem in the media and in the health care marketplace. Concierge Medicine, also known as "Direct Care" and sometimes aligned with terms such as: Direct Primary Care; Membership Medicine; Boutique Medicine; Retainer-Based Medicine; Elitist Medicine; Concierge Health Care; Cash-Only Practice; Direct Practice Medicine And One Of My Laughable Favorites, Wealth-Care.

In general, the term Concierge Medicine is used to describe a direct relationship between a patient and a primary care physician in which the patient pays a fee for access and care from their primary care doctor. In today's marketplace, the role of Concierge Medicine is an important one because it will help shape the 'other' side of healthcare in our country in the coming years ahead.

As we've seen the polarization of the nation's two political parties, so we've seen the antithetical positions established between insured healthcare and private pay medicine in America. Throughout the past decade and since the emergence of Concierge Medicine in the mid-1990's, Concierge Medicine has been identified as a selfishly practiced business model run by financially-focused physicians, who abandon their patients for dollars. The more recent Summer 2012 Supreme Court Ruling on Obamacare does little to unite these two contrasting medical practice philosophies together – but widens the gap between them even more.

It is a little known fact that over ninety percent (90%) of current concierge physicians across the U.S. need additional patients in order to reach their desired patient threshold, according to a survey conducted by The Concierge Medicine Research

Collective in 2010 ("The Collective"). The Collective also found that nearly twenty percent (20%) of concierge physicians who start a concierge medical practice try and fail in the first two years. The resulting aftermath involves having to re-brand their practice to the more familiar insurance-based, managed care business model. When these physicians were asked what caused their downfall they reported 'not enough patient interest.'

On the positive-side, based upon our experience and the data our organizations have compiled over the years, Concierge Medicine has a long, relational history with its patients. The likelihood of one patient to stay with the same concierge doctor is averaging seven to nine years versus the traditional insurance-based or managed care doctor who averages only five to seven years patient retention.

All of this data is meant to be encouraging to you as you grow your practice and build your brand in your local area. This concept or trend, initially thought of by many as healthcare for the rich – is now accessible and quite affordable for couples, seniors on Medicare, young families and individuals with or without healthcare. We will outline the supporting data of this in the chapters ahead.

In the next few chapters, we are going to explore the popularity of Concierge Medicine. We will look at polling data and surveys conducted inside these medical practices and how they are growing throughout the United States and abroad. We'll also outline the specific marketing and branding strategies being used, both online and offline, and how your concierge medical practice can reinforce and communicate the benefits of your practice to current and prospective patients in your local area.

We have also got some surprises for you and a bonus Q and A from concierge physician and Facebook maven, Dr. Shira Miller – the first female concierge physician to reach more than 10,000 Fans with her Medical Practice Facebook Page.

So, fasten your seatbelts, turn your cell phones to airplane mode and let's begin!

CHAPTER 1

YOUR PRACTICE IS MORE

THAN JUST 'A TREND.'

CHAPTER 1

YOUR PRACTICE IS MORE
THAN JUST 'A TREND.'

In Thomas Goetz's article *"How To Spot The Future"* published in April 2012 edition of WIRED, he outlined seven principles that underlie many of our contemporary innovations. He states..."Odds are that any idea we deem potentially transformative, any trend we think has legs, draws on one or more of these core principles. They have played a major part in creating the world we see today. And they'll be the forces behind the world we'll be living in tomorrow."

Here is an excerpt from his article that I believe helps identify Concierge Medicine as more than just a here today – gone tomorrow innovation. Goetz continues..."First, look for cross-pollinators. It's no secret that the best ideas—the ones with the most impact and longevity—are transferable; an innovation in one industry can be exported to transform another. But even more resonant are those ideas that are cross-disciplinary not just in their application but in their origin."

The vitality we see in today's Concierge Medicine marketplace resulted from the recognition that long wait times, overburdened physicians and insurance companies aren't exclusive to the practice of medicine. In the past two decades, doctors have gone from occasionally emailing, phoning or texting a patient and using Skype and the iPhone camera for dispatching medical advice to opening up successful practices and there — eagerly incorporating ideas such as Marcus Welby-style home visits, modern-day information technology and prescription writing methods into their medical bag. When concierge doctors talk about medicine being "the oldest new form of medicine," they're not speaking figuratively—they are trying to reframe the identity of their practice and the industry. As Goetz says, ... "that's testimony to a wave of cross-pollination that will blur the line between personal electronics and automobiles."

If you'd like to read Goetz's entire WIRED article, visit

http://www.wired.com/business/2012/04/ff_spotfutu re/all/.

When Concierge Medicine Today and it's research and data collection arm, *The Concierge Medicine Research Collective* (herein "The Collective") asked currently practicing concierge physician offices (June 2009 – July 2012) how long it takes to recruit one new patient into their practices, surveys indicated the following:

- 49% – Four Plus Months (4+ Mos.) of concierge physician offices say it takes more than four months to recruit a new patient.

- 23% – Three Plus Months (3+ Mos.) of concierge physician offices say it takes more than three months to recruit a new patient.

- 4% – Two Plus Months (2+ Mos.) of concierge physician offices say it takes more than two months to recruit a new patient.

- 12% – Two to Three Weeks Plus (2 to 3+ Weeks) of concierge physician offices say it takes more than two to three weeks to recruit a new patient.

- 12% – One to Two Weeks Plus (1 to 2+ Weeks) of concierge physician offices say it takes more than one to two weeks to recruit a new patient.

Concierge Medicine Today also revealed that utilizing a blended rate based upon national averages for current fees charged for concierge medical care, an estimated 9,285,714,286 people could be provided concierge medical care with the [at that time] 13 trillion dollar national debt. Carrying this out 928,571,429 people could be provided this care for 10 years. These figures are based upon information obtained through average pricing surveys conducted by Concierge Medicine Today from 2009-2010.

As we have discussed, Concierge Medicine is a relatively young, but proven business model and deserves to be examined in more detail. One would presume that if a physician unlocks their practice doors and puts a sign outside that naturally, people would come. The popular movie line 'If you build it they will come,' was fantastic for a corn farmer in Iowa but it's a lousy marketing strategy.

According to polls from Concierge Medicine Today (2009 to 2012), found that patient retention inside a concierge medical practice is between 84 and 96 percent. Broken down, this means a concierge physician with at least two years of experience in the marketplace is able to retain up to ninety-six (96%) of his or her patients each year. That's a great track-record for a relatively new business model.

When you combine a high-deductible or catastrophic health plan policy with a concierge medical program you empower people and families to make better decisions about their health care. They in turn, receive more comprehensive medical care and then the savings happen. Stronger relationships occur between the physician and their patients. One successful California concierge doctor stated it this way when she says that her patients now say... "I no longer have a doctor who needs to look at a chart to know my name."

But let's take a look at the inside of a typical internist or family physician practice. Their practice can carry a patient load of 2,500+ patients whereas a concierge physician generally limits their practice to between 300-600 patients or so. While all Concierge Medicine practices share similarities, they vary widely in their structure, payment requirements, and form of operation. In particular, they differ in the level of service provided and the amount of the fee charged. Concierge physicians usually charge patients an annual fee ranging from $600 (dependent on services offered) to $1,800/year. In some rare cases, a much higher fee is charged, which the media has predetermined as the norm. In exchange for this affordable fee though, concierge practices generally include 24/7 access to a personal physicians' cell phone, same-day appointments with no waiting, personal coordination of care with specialists, personal follow up when admitted to a hospital or ER, house calls, and more.

According to another survey conducted by The Collective from 2010-2011, when concierge physicians were asked what is their greatest challenge when recruiting a new patient each year?' physicians said the following:

- 59% - Educating new, prospective patients about the benefits of their practice is their greatest challenge.

- 33% - Losing existing patients when transitioning to the Concierge Medicine model due to pricing is their greatest challenge; and

- 8% - said starting a concierge practice with no patients from scratch was their greatest challenge.

So, how do physicians with a great business model and emerging market grow their practice?

First, let's look at the real cost of concierge medical care in the U.S. Concierge Medicine Today found that from 2007 to 2012, over sixty percent (60%) of concierge medical programs across the U.S. cost the individual less than $135 per month. In some cases, care programs cost as little as $10 per month for children. A doctor in Wichita, Kansas, one of the first concierge medical practices in

Wichita, offers flat monthly fees, age-banded which range from $10 per month for kids and $50, $75 or $100 per month for adults. Members of this same practice receive unlimited access to their doctor at their home, work or doctor's office along with unlimited 'technology visits' such as cell phone calls, web cam visits, email and texting.

Furthermore, many concierge physicians across the U.S. offer their patients access to wholesaie pricing on prescriptions, lab tests, vaccinations, popular shots, imaging services and medical supplies, passing on pre-negotiated discounts to patients.

CHAPTER 2

WHY SHOULD PEOPLE
CHOOSE CONCIERGE MEDICINE?
AND NO, IT'S NOT PRICE.

CHAPTER 2

WHY SHOULD PEOPLE
CHOOSE CONCIERGE MEDICINE?
AND NO, IT'S NOT PRICE.

A recent story in the New York Times supports this belief. The paper reports that the State of Indiana offers both a high-deductible plan and a traditional HMO. People in the high-deductible plan spend thousands less than those in the HMO.

"The average expense in 2009 for patients on one of these [high-deductible] plans was $6,393," the paper writes, "compared with $8,570 for patients enrolled in a more traditional health maintenance organization plan."

Responses and opinions may vary to this data but one thing is for certain, concierge medical care in the U.S. is affordable. Too often, this message is not carried into a physician's marketing messaging or communicated to his or her staff.

The following data about concierge medical practices in the U.S. and Canada may be surprising but it's important to know and understand as you craft the brand and message for your practice's future marketing activities.

The Collective in coordination with Concierge Medicine Today recently asked patients of concierge medical care providers 'Why do you choose Concierge Medicine?' The answers may be a surprise to some of you:

- 34% said price compared to value received was the main reason they chose concierge medical care;

- 17% said Medicare acceptance/participation was the main reason;

- 6% said more time with the doctor;

- 2% said limited or no waiting;

- 6% said less office staff to deal with;

- and 29% said insurance compatibility was the main reason they chose concierge medical care.

The takeaway here is that while proper pricing is important, it's the additional features and benefits that help build your personal brand and make you more attractive to prospective patients in your local area. The second takeaway here and important to understand is that what you think is important isn't always the most important thing to your patients. A lot of concierge practice marketing materials that I see emphasizes more time with the doctor and limited or no waiting. These aren't even in the top 3 as to why patients choose this type of care!

EXECUTIVES ARE NOT THE BEST TARGETS FOR CONCIERGE MEDICINE.

Despite high-powered executives touting that they use Concierge Medicine, executives of all ages and backgrounds are not the most popular patient demographic searching and using this type of health care.

According to Concierge Medicine Today's research, surveys and polling data, Concierge Medicine patients throughout the U.S. show that top level executives and celebrities account for less than six (6%) percent of concierge medical patients across America.

So, with the number of consultants and people in the marketplace saying you should target your marketing efforts towards these prospective patients, I would caution you and tell you to evaluate carefully the amount of dollars you allocate to this audience. While they may still be part of your overall long-term marketing strategy, a lot of physicians have come to the obvious conclusion that this audience is not necessarily their primary target market.

So, if it's not executives, who is the primary audience searching for concierge medical care? Well, Concierge Medicine Today's very popular DOC-FINDER search engine data reveals the following:

- 49% of all concierge physician searches are from individuals;
- 23% of all concierge physician searches are from couples with no children;
- 21% of all concierge physician searches are from families with children;

Based upon this data, one can conclude that concierge medical care is once again, not simply for the deep pocketed executives or celebrities. In fact, data tells us that over 50% of the people using concierge medical care earn a combined household income of less than $100,000 per year.

CHAPTER 3

Foundational Principles of Effective Marketing To Grow Your Practice.

CHAPTER 3

Foundational Principles of Effective Marketing To Grow Your Practice.

I personally believe that if more people are exposed to the affordable cost information and coordinated value of a particular concierge practice near their work or home that it would make a tremendous difference in what they spend each year on health care. That being said, I understand that it's not easy to grow a business in today's economy. Marketing is becoming more mature, wouldn't you agree?

A friend and marketing colleague of mine recently told me at lunch the other day 'the goal of any marketing program, whether online or thru print, is to create sign-posts in the places where your customers (i.e. prospective patients) travel. Pattern interrupts, if you will. Then, if we've done our job correctly, we direct that traffic to the business for more information.' I couldn't agree more...!

PRINCIPLE # 1
LEARN FROM THOSE COMPANIES WITH THE GREATEST AMOUNT of SUCCESS.

"

There is a lot to learn from those pioneers who ventured into an uncertain marketplace before you. Take advantage of that knowledge, educate yourself and most importantly, you'll have potentially learned what not to do in your practice.

"

PRINCIPLE # 1
LEARN FROM THOSE COMPANIES WITH THE GREATEST AMOUNT of SUCCESS.

At some point in your business, a marketing consultant, salesman or saleswoman, may approach you and promise you the world. Maybe you've already bought into it and are skeptical of marketing altogether. However, it's at this point in time where I remind you that the first principle of effective concierge medical marketing is 'Learn From Those Companies With The Greatest Amount of Success.'

Following this principle means looking at what the men and women around you and in your industry are doing to grow their business. They've obviously found some success in your local area or market and have spent a considerable amount of time and money to get where they are today. Learn from what they have done. Look at their Facebook Page, their web site, brochures, office design, etc.

There is a lot to learn from those pioneers who ventured into an uncertain marketplace before you. Take advantage of that knowledge, educate yourself and most importantly, you'll have potentially learned what not to do in your practice.

From 2009 to the writing and compilation of this audio series and book, October of 2012, The Collective asked concierge physicians what form of marketing they found to work best to grow their patient-base. The results were as follows:

- 7% use Facebook to grow their practice and get new patients.
- 2% use Twitter to grow their practice and get new patients.
- 5% use postcards to grow their practice and get new patients.
- 5% use a letter alone, to grow their practice and get new patients.
- 18% use a letter with a brochure about their practice and get new patients.

- 21% say hiring a marketing/PR company that used both online and offline marketing strategies helped grow their practice and generate new patients.

- 3% say hiring a practice management consultant to organize internal processes grew their practice and obtained a few new patients.

- 9% participate in local area networking activities and events.

- 16% say local area advertising combined with low-risk offers helped grow their practice; and

- 14% say word of mouth from existing patients helped to grow their practice.

If some of you reading or hearing this audio book now presume that using a Yellow Page ad, talking to patients more and putting an ad in your local newspaper for a month is the right method of marketing and branding your practice – you've missed the first principle of effective concierge medical marketing which is 'Follow Those With The

Greatest Amount of Success.' Learn from what your successful colleagues have done and blaze a trail that's unique but similar to those with the most success.

What's critical that we focus on when examining this data is that the MAJORITY of smart, well-educated physicians found that the best and fastest way to grow their concierge medical practice was to hire a marketing and PR company that uses both offline and online marketing strategies to grow their practice. This will include all of the following ideas as well as revisiting your practice web site, your social media strategy and developing great low-risk offers for your practice.

We're living in unprecedented times. We are probably preaching to the choir for many of you, but here's the thing. When marketing and branding your practice in social media, there is no middle-man. The playing field is leveled. Everybody has the opportunity to build their own Profile and pages and grow their own business.

However, a little caveat for you – and that's why I wrote this book. It's very, very noisy out there so how do you stand out? How do you reach your target audience without wasting a lot of time sitting in front of your computer for hours on end with chatting, friending and liking?

I know fear actually stops a lot of people. Fear of making a mistake. Fear of being exposed or having your privacy invaded and the like. And guess what? Did you know the number one fear that stops businesses from building a really significant brand or presence on Facebook is fear of negative comments? Can you believe that?

My personal opinion and that of other social media and branding strategists is that when you receive a negative comment out in public, that that's a great opportunity to demonstrate stellar customer service right out in the open. Turn the situation around. Act promptly and you could very well end up having a patient for life, and having many, many people observe the wonderful attention that you gave the situation is powerful 'word of mouth marketing.'

So, don't be afraid of negative comments. Build up a nice positive culture. From time to time you'll receive negative comments, but deal with it in the moment promptly and courteously, and give people the benefit of the doubt.

One other important note I'd like to mention on the topic of Facebook. Social Media mogul, Gary Vaynerchuk call social media "word of mouth marketing on steroids," and of course Facebook is the number one social network. Facebook marketing expert Mari Smith and her team gets very excited about is all of these different sites working together qualify and generate new prospective patient leads and inquiries for physicians. Mari continues to note, "Facebook is leading the way but social media inserted into your overall marketing budget and strategy is so important moving forward. Social media is creating massive shifts and changing the way we 'do' marketing. "

As we close Principle # 1, LEARN FROM THOSE COMPANIES WITH THE GREATEST AMOUNT of SUCCESS, I want you to know that you don't need to be intimidated by all the different social media platforms. You don't need 27 thousand fans. You don't even need 2,700 fans. There are plenty of successful businesses that have small fan pages. I think a lot of people get concerned and may be thinking, 'what can I learn from a major brand?' I think you can learn a lot, but the thing is, what if you only had 500 or 5,000 genuine fans on Facebook or Google+ or Twitter? When they engage, they love you, they in turn, spread and share their love for your practice or brand with their friends. And what if you could create that in 100 Days? We'll share more about a special program with you at the end [I.e. Chapter 6 and 7] but for now, let's keep on going with the helpful information for your practice.

CHAPTER 4

PRINCIPLE #2

THE LOW-RISK, IRRESISTIBLE OFFER.

"

*If You Have Something
Good To Say, Say It
Well and Say It Often.*

"

PRINCIPLE #2

THE LOW-RISK, IRRESISTIBLE OFFER.

As a marketing consultant for the concierge medical community as well as a health care marketing and PR strategist for many years, the biggest, singular mistake I see physicians make is...they don't have an irresistible low-risk offer for the prospective patient that entices them to want to take the next step and learn more about their practice, it's products, services or people.

A low-risk or irresistible offer is usually something free for the prospective patient or reader of your email, web site or advertisement. It can be a coupon, a free book, a checklist, a free DVD, and is usually a free 'something' that engages and entices the reader to want to know more about who you are and what you are selling.

As a fundraising and marketing consultant for non-profits, one of the strategies I consistently communicate to our designers and writers is 'give the reader something free and ask them for their money.' It's common sense. Just about everyone will give you their email address or call a toll-free number to get something free. If you make it easy to get 'something of value' for free, free being a clearly communicated word, people inevitably will take you up on it. Then, you know you've 'qualified' a lead and can start accumulating a clearer message to those now showing interest in your practice.

Some offers are easy: "Bring this coupon in and get a free cup of coffee." But others get to be more complicated. It's difficult to sell certain products or services by simply saying, "this is what it does," and "you get $20 off." Those are offers that we refer to in the marketing world as a platitude. One example we're all familiar with is 'we provide high-quality service' or 'we've been in the business since...'. Webster's Dictionary defines platitude as a remark or statement, that has been used too often to be interesting or thoughtful.

In the concierge medical community, your service requires not only an investment of my time but also a long-term, (although some offices have month-to-month contracts with their patients), investment of dollars. If I understand my healthcare coverage to be sufficient and I am covered by my insurance premiums that I'm already paying, why should I pay a few extra dollars out-of-pocket to see you. One might be willing to wait in line to see the doctor if it doesn't cost them more money, right?

Well, the more costly the service or product, the more a prospective patient wants a lot more information before making a buying decision. These prospects might need an educational meeting, a brochure, a personal letter from the doctor accompanied by a phone call from someone of prominence in the practice or maybe even a short webinar. Instead of providing them with generic platitudes, provide them with a low-risk/irresistible, free offer to help them get to know, like and trust you even more.

Some examples of a low-risk offer could be:

- This Free Report changes everything; Learn why your insurance may not be working for you!

- Exam, X-Rays and Flu Shot – $150 Adults - $100 Kids!

- Enter Your Name and Email Address for a Special coupon and FREE ALLERGY CHECKLIST

- Spring Special! $250 Off 6 and 12-Month Memberships

- Get Your Fourth Month FREE!

- $250 off, $350 senior citizens/U.S. Military Personnel discount

- Free Physician Consultation and Body Fat Analysis (a $500 Value!), FREE!

NOTE: Each of the above low-risk offers are examples to be used as a reference. You should consult your marketing team and possibly your attorney if you believe any offer you develop may not be in accordance with local or state laws. It's also important to note that your low-risk offer needs to be tailored to your practice specifically and your targeted local audience.

I'm going to share a simple, secret strategy with you right now. It's very strategic and you must start thinking of your marketing and messaging in a different way as you move forward and grow your patient-base. When I'm making posts on Facebook, Twitter, LinkedIn, etc., I'm always thinking about building value and having people engage with me online. Then, at some point I'll drop a little status update, "Check out my Fan Page." As you'll learn in the next section, THE VALUE LADDER, you've got to start building value with the prospective patient-base around your practice who know nothing about you.

When you build value overtime, they will begin to know, like and trust you – and eventually want to do business with you!

CHAPTER 5

PRINCIPLE # 3 – THE VALUE LADDER.

"

"You create an irresistible offer to bring someone into your value ladder. If your customer receives value from you at that point, they will naturally want to ascend up to be able to receive more value from you."

~Russell Brunson

"

PRINCIPLE # 3 – THE VALUE LADDER.

In every business there are always people who will purchase just about anything you are selling, right? You've probably noticed this in your own practice. There are usually a limited number of patients who will most likely buy anything you sell to them. Their perceived value in your and your services matches the price point your offering.

Then there are those patients who need a little more information and persuasion. This audience is aware of your services, history, reputation, etc., and eventually, they'll purchase something from you -- with just a little extra effort on your part and some patience.

Last, there's always a significant portion of a practice that always wants something for free or deeply discounted. They don't know you or trust you yet...so you've got to build trust with them so that in turn, they'll begin to know, like and trust you in the near future.

The same principle holds true when developing the value ladder for your concierge medical practice. You start at the bottom of the ladder with a free, low-risk, no-obligation offer. This engages and interrupts your prospective audience and qualifies them as part of your next step of the ladder. Meaning, if they took advantage of your free-offer, maybe they'll come to our meet-and-greet with the doctor next month?

In an article by Internet Multi-Millionaire Russell Brunson, he states "You create an irresistible offer to bring someone into your value ladder. If your customer receives value from you at that point, they will naturally want to ascend up to be able to receive more value from you."

Therefore, after a person that you've identified as a prospect begins to walk up your very own practice's value ladder, you wouldn't immediately try to sell them your $1,800 membership or care plan would you? If the answer is no, you're beginning to understand how the value ladder works. If your answer was yes, well, this book will enlighten you.

As you can see, the more perceived value your current patients and prospective patients receive, the higher price point they will be willing to pay. Educational articles and low-risk offers help nurture this a lot. Are patients upset that they have to pay their doctor more money after they've received an irresistible offer from you or they've been with you for a couple years? No. They are typically happy that you were able to see their problem and promptly fix it.

Very few concierge medical practices that we have seen have ever diagramed out step-by-step where they are trying to take their prospective patients and current patients after they respond to one of their offers. They normally are so excited to have a new patient that they start trying to sell them everything, or worse, they get so nervous that they don't sell them anything.

You have probably read articles online or heard stories about businesses who have used companies like Groupon, Loclly and Living Social, and they will get 50, 100 or more customers in a one day or one week. They then complain and say that they lost money by running the offer. Brunson continues by saying "those companies who are complaining are the same companies who haven't thought through their value ladder."

"When you create your value ladder, you can predictably know how much money you will make for every person who requests your irresistible offer," Brunson adds. "You will also know on average how much money you can make from each of these customers and you'll know the lifetime value of those customers."

By now, you've probably started to see how the Value Ladder works and how it is so critical to construct before you move ahead with future marketing activities, correct? If you think you may need help constructing your own Value Ladder or Low-Risk Offer, I'm going to share some details with you at the end of this book and audio series [i.e. the Chapter 6] that can help you take the next steps and provide you some additional resources to get you moving in the days and weeks ahead.

"

Dental and Pediatric
'Concierge' Practices ... On The Rise

According to Concierge Medicine Today's recently released research which analyzed concierge medicine specialties across the country for the past 12 months, over 66% of current concierge physician practices operating today across the U.S. are primarily 'internal medicine.'

A surprising finding in this study was the increasing number of concierge 'dental' and 'pediatric' practices arising since February of 2009 to August 2012.

Source: www.AskTheCollective.org

"

CHAPTER 6

**PRINCIPLE #4
A LEAD GENERATING WEB SITE vs.
A BROCHURE WEB SITE.**

> **There are generally two types of web site designs being constructed these days. It's critical to understand the difference between the two when considering building or re-designing your current site...**

PRINCIPLE #4
A LEAD GENERATING WEB SITE vs.
A BROCHURE WEB SITE.

There are generally two types of web site designs being constructed these days. It's critical to understand the difference between the two when considering building or re-designing your current site...especially if you are interested in a positive return on your investment.

The two types of web sites are a **Brochure Web Site** and a **Marketing Web Site**. Now the common misconception is assuming by having a web site at all is that it qualifies as part of your marketing efforts. That is simply not the case and is important to understand as it applies to the fundamental principle differences between marketing and advertising.

The Brochure Web Site.

Also called 'a pretty web site,' the Brochure Web Site's primary function is to simply educate the visitor [i.e. prospective patient] on the services, products and history of your practice. Or, sometimes provide resources exclusively for the purpose of branding. We call it a brochure web site because it is really no more than a glorified electronic version of your practice brochure.

While brochure web sites can play a role in your business to verify your practice's existence for a-would-be prospective patient, there should be little expectation that it will be a significant part of your overall marketing. For the overall positioning is about the company itself and not on the prospective patients' needs nor provides a compelling reason [i.e. Low-Risk Offer] for that visitor to take an action which is at the heart of a "Marketing Web Site."

The Marketing Web Site.

The Marketing Web Site has one mission that IS critical to your business. That is to attract interested visitors to your site and convert/qualify them as prospects to create the opportunity for more future patients.

The Marketing Web Site is all about having the visitor take a specific action that you decide upon. It can involve signing up for an event, calling a number or entering information such as name and email in exchange for: an informational article or newsletter, CD, DVD, checklist, free report or video of value and substance that has relevant information of interest to the prospective patient. That is essential to the overall strategy and Value Ladder in order to grow your practice.

Remember, the ultimate goal of a marketing web site is to generate and qualify new leads and business opportunities for the online success of your practice. As doctors begin to look at their web sites more analytically, most will find they have brochure web sites not marketing web sites.

The question you should ask yourself if you don't have a web site at all is...'do you want a brochure website, or one that generates more customers and makes you money...or both?'

I actually have a handy marketing tool for you called the "Social Media Cheat Sheet." I call it a cheat sheet because after several years of instructing, teaching and consulting with businesses, like yours, it has exactly what you need to do and where you need to go to get started building your brand on the most important social media platforms. You can find that in the SHOP tab or Marketing Section of our web site, www.ConciergeMedicineToday.com.

CHAPTER 7

PRINCIPLE #5

YOUR FOLLOW UP SYSTEM.

"

What good is a new lead or new prospective patient from your web site or direct mail program [to your practice] if you never call, email or follow-up with them about their inquiry?

"

PRINCIPLE #5
YOUR FOLLOW UP SYSTEM.

Patient retention figures collected by Concierge Medicine Today have been consistent since the year 2000. However we are finding that these retention numbers are beginning to steadily decline due to one major factor – some doctors [and staff] are over-promising and under-delivering on the care and service they provide. This in turn, leaves patients unsatisfied. On the positive side, these patients leaving their current concierge doctor are overwhelmingly still selecting to use Concierge Medicine, albeit from another physician in their local area.

What good is a new lead or new prospective patient to your practice if you never call, email or send them information about your practice? Everyone wants to communicate differently these days. And, if you have followed the Principles of Effective Concierge Medical Marketing outlined here, you will soon find that 'The Fortune Is In The Follow-Up!'

For example, if you have someone who visits your "Marketing Web Site" and you've clearly communicated your low-risk offer to them, they in turn, are beginning to know, like and trust you. Soon, with the appropriate follow-up and strategic use of your value ladder messages, you will be able to turn these prospective patients into paying patients. But, it's critical to understand that not everyone likes to be communicated with in the same way. Therefore, having a strong auto-generated email program in place to email your growing list is important. Having a strong Facebook Business Page with regular, daily posts is also important. Some people like receiving special offers via SMS text messages.

The important thing to remember is that when you begin to follow-up with these people over and over again and you are consistently showing them value via the strategic low-risk offers or information you've developed, they will begin to find value in you and your practice too!

CHAPTER 8

SO WHAT DO I DO NOW?

UNDERSTANDING THE REAL COST OF

ACQUIRING A NEW CUSTOMER AND

KNOWING WHAT THE RIGHT

NEXT STEP IS.

CHAPTER 8

SO WHAT DO I DO NOW? UNDERSTANDING THE REAL COST OF ACQUIRING A NEW CUSTOMER AND KNOWING WHAT THE RIGHT NEXT STEP IS.

Russell Brunson of DotComSecrets in a recent online article writes "The battle of marketing against your competition will always come down to one thing. Who can spend the most to acquire a new customer? The business with the biggest wallet is not the business who is going to win this battle. The business with the strongest value ladder will always win."

Source: http://www.dotcomsecrets.com/your-value-ladder/

Most people already have a reference for TV, radio and print costs but not so much for online marketing. U.S. Bancorp's Piper Jaffray conducted an interesting breakdown of the estimated average cost of acquiring a new customer using varied mediums. Combining this research with McKinsey and Company's estimates, the calculated price-tag for each new customer looks like this:

- $230 per customer thru Television Advertising
- $125 per customer thru Specialty Magazines
- $70 per customer thru Direct Mail Campaigns
- $20 per customer thru Print (i.e. Yellow Pages)
- $8.50 per customer thru Internet (i.e. Google, SEO, Ad Words, Facebook, Etc.)

If you're wondering where to get started, I'd suggest examining other marketing channels to expand your reach. The best part is, for the most part, they're free!

First, you might have created other social channels that you're not currently using for business purposes. Twitter, Google+, LinkedIn, YouTube, Friendster, Pinterest. All of these are great social media platforms for marketing your practice. You might also have another channel like your own blog subscribers or your email list.

Second, if you have a local business, a physical establishment, think about the eyeballs of your current patients. What are they reading when they are inside your practice? Here's a bonus tip for you – if you have a local office that you see patients at, look at the pieces of literature and brochures you are using to promote various programs, events and your practice. It never ceases to amaze me how so many doctors' offices don't put their social channels on their business cards, brochures, eye-level on the internal door(s) as they exit, in the restroom, etc.

Simply putting a statement "Come and chat with us on Facebook" will help your users engage with your brand online. And, there's no better time to get them to like your page or say something positive about their most recent visit with you than while they are thinking about it. Place your social media channel logos and a simple phrase on your window signage, decals on windows or mirrors, walls, cash register or right on the products or forms you give to current patients.

MOBILE MARKETING.

I love mobile marketing because it's so fast and easy to engage with a brand on my smart phone and tablet. One marketing tool we suggest concierge physicians and their staff take advantage of is check-ins on Facebook and SMS (Short Message Service, that's texting). Every person that walks into your practice or is even in the vicinity of your office could pick you up on their GPS or smart phone. They're a hot prospect for you. Even if you have a practice based out of your home and you provide mainly home visits to your patients, you've got tons and tons of ways that you can draw people (i.e. prospective patients) in to get more engagement with your practice and brand in social media.

EMBRACE FACEBOOK "CHECK-INS" …
They're Just Like Word of Mouth
Referrals FOR every MEDICAL PRACTICE.

Virtually every brand and business today has a Facebook Page. Unfortunately, medical practices are one of the last to adopt-a-page and jump into the social media-sphere. As most people are looking to fill idle time with smart phone usage, few medical practices have made their Facebook Business Page "local." All that practices have to do to make their Page "local" is to add an address to their Facebook Page settings.

Once an address is added, Facebook users will be able to check-in by either tagging their location in a post or by navigating to your page and clicking "check-in." Note that users must be within a certain radius before the "check-in" button will appear. tip; Make sure to change your Facebook Page "type" to "BRAND" or "LOCAL BUSINESS" in order to enable users to check-in. Otherwise, some Page types will not have an option to add an address.

"

If someone lives near your medical practice and Google's your name or practice name, will your practice name, address, telephone, map to your office and web site show up on Google? If not, you are missing out on one of the easiest and most cost effective way to attract patients to your practice. Placing your practice on Google Maps is free and takes only minutes to submit your information.

Go to: maps.google.com

"

CHAPTER 9

QUICK TIPS and Q and A From Experts

and

Concierge Physicians, Like You.

CHAPTER 9

QUICK TIPS and Q and A From Experts and Physicians, Like You.

SINGLE-SERVE BREW STATIONS MAKING BIG IMPRESSIONS WITH CONCIERGE PATIENTS.

Occasionally you might run out of the house without your hot cup of tea or favorite blend of coffee at your side. If you're like me, you love the convenience of a fresh, cup of tea or coffee when you're running late.

The Keurig K-Cup coffee makers and other single-serve and pod coffee/tea brewers have come into businesses with a flury of excitement over the past two years. Patients spending any amount of time in your office will appreciate the convenience and employees of concierge medical practices love the easy, no mess -- clean up they provide.

In recent months, these single coffee cup brewers have become much more affordable and stylish.

Some of the larger big-box wholesale clubs even sell such devices to their members with 60 or more K-Cups included with the price of the coffee maker. So, if you have the traditional-style coffee maker which involves making a full pot of coffee, you're behind the trend...!

REFRESHMENT SERVICE TIPS FOR YOUR CONCIERGE PRACTICE

- Keep a fresh assortment of tea and coffee flavors -- don't limit your lobby coffee maker to one or two flavors.

- Have one of your staff monitor the water tank twice a day (or more, in some cases) and fill the water tank with filtered or distilled water routinely.

- Use throw-away, to-go cups with lids. Lids show that you've gone the extra mile to provide convenience for your patients -- plus, it helps prevents spills around the office!

- Don't bring out the old coffee mugs from the break area.

- We all know the health factors that go along with drinking soda. Because you're trying to promote good health, only in rare circumstances, offer soda to your guests if they ask for them. Have them chilled inside a small refrigerator in your lobby or in the break room.
- Have chilled, bottled water readily available for your patients.

TWITTER FOR PHYSICIANS

When sending a tweet out into the oblivion, you are actually sending it out only to those who have chosen in return to follow YOU. The benefit of having "Followers" means you are communicating with an audience who finds what you have to say interesting. If they find it really interesting, they will "RT" or "ReTweet" it to their "Followers." And so the cycle can continue on and on. What's the benefit? Maximum exposure for you and if you've done your marketing right, maximum exposure for your brand and a data collection center at your web site!

So, when is the best time to send out a tweet? Should you send it out during the day or night or both? There are plenty of reports and analysis out there as to when the best time to tweet is.. so you might find some of these tips useful when it comes to tweeting at the best possible time.

"

*By 2015, More People Will Be
Using Their Mobile Devices To
Access The Internet Than
Computers*
(Source: Quantcast, 2010)

*Submission And Optimization To
The Various Mapping Platforms
On The Web Today, Will Provide
Users With The Ability To Quickly
Gps Your Location Via Their
Mobile Device Or Computer.*

"

FACEBOOK FOR PHYSICIANS

When concierge physicians across the U.S. and Canada were asked 'Do you use Facebook to communicate and connect with your patients?' the survey indicated to us that:

- 67% DO NOT use Facebook in any business capacity whatsoever;
- 30% said YES! They do use Facebook for business purposes.
- That remaining 3% said they have created a Facebook Business page but abandoned it due to lack of the right skillsets necessary to update it regularly.

PREPARE A TABLET STRATEGY

FOR YOUR PRACTICE

More and more people are using tablets like the iPad to surf the web during business hours, waiting rooms, meetings and at home. Searches among tablet users have increased exponentially in the past year and more PR agencies and small business promoters are encouraging business owners to stay updated in the latest technology trends by creating web sites, blogs and geo-targeted advertisements specific for tablets. This also includes the use of videos. So, while creating a tablet marketing strategy for your practice might seem like a time vacuum, it would be wise for you to consider talking to a web professional to help you prepare for the next phase in social connection.

"

When your prospect sees your practice (or name) in multiple places online, you are perceived to be the expert. They will begin to feel like they have spent lots of time with you. This allows them to know, like, and trust you faster, resulting in quicker patient referrals, visits, appointments and purchases.

"

The Fundamental Four

There are just four Social Marketing platforms that you can leverage as sign posts directing traffic to your articles.

Facebook

Create a Fan Page on Facebook. Announce to your fans when you are working on a new article. This builds anticipation for your article. Then when your article is done and published on your blog or EzineArticles, post the title of your article with a link back to your article. You could have a regular feature on your Fan Page where on a certain day of the week you publish a new article link.

YouTube

With todays' technology and tools, you can quickly and easily create Video Articles out of your best articles and upload them to YouTube. We were raised on TV and YouTube is just another version of that powerful screen. Use it. Be sure to include a link to the original article in the description of your video.

Twitter

Twitter is a gold mine for redirecting traffic to your articles. Once a new article is out, either on your blog or on an Article Directory, announce that the article is available. Then make multiple follow up announcements throughout the next few days as well. Use quotes from your article and include the link. Ask "Have you seen this yet?" and direct them to your article.

The thing to remember about Twitter is that it is very fluid. So an announcement you make one day in the morning might not be seen by someone who will see a similar announcement that you make the next afternoon.

LinkedIn

As you know, each social media tool has its own personality. Facebook is a lot like the local pub. A pub is a place where you can go in, chat with friends, tell a few jokes and relax a little bit. This is essentially why Facebook usually falls on the distraction side of time spent on the Internet. But, **LinkedIn is more like a trade show** -- as in a place where you'd keep things pretty buttoned-up and formalized. No need to mention your vacation in Las Vegas on LinkedIn. But that white paper you wrote? Perfect for LinkedIn!

"

Listing sites such as Switchboard.com, Yahoo!, Bing, Google Local, YP.com, Kudzu.com and AngiesList.com allows searchers to narrow their search by categories of services. It would make sense to take the time to tie your services to as many of these categories as possible so that your practice appears in more instances when a person is searching.

"

In November of 2011, *Concierge Medicine Today*
Interviewed Dr. Shira Miller -- Facebook's First Concierge Physician To Reach More Than 10,000+ Followers!

As Concierge Medicine Today caught up with Dr. Shira Miller, Founder and Medical Director of The Integrative Center for Health & Wellness, a concierge menopause, post menopause, and anti-aging practice for men and women -- We asked her some important questions pertaining to the topic of social media and marketing a concierge practice online. Topics also covered included her success on Facebook, email and what she does to attract new patients to her practice. Here's what she had to say...

CMT [Editor, Michael]: What tips, tricks, message crafting concepts, etc., would you give to other [concierge] physicians considering using social media to help attract new patients?

DR. MILLER: I believe that social media is a great way for prospective patients to learn of your existence and get to know your expertise in a non-threatening and non-committed environment. Then, if they like you and trust you and need a doctor like you, they are more likely to choose you.

CMT [Editor, Michael]: Would you suggest only it (i.e. Facebook) for [marketing to] your current patients?

DR. MILLER: No way. My patients get inside info and special treatment that is not available on Facebook. And, the main reason I use FB is to gain exposure and educate people who are not my patients. My current patients already know me and what I do, and I know them, and we have each other's email addresses which allows for most excellent communication. Don't get me wrong, many of my patients are my FB fans and they continue to learn through my updates and help share my information with their friends, but they are the minority. I also use Twitter and LinkedIn.

CMT [Editor, Michael]: Would you encourage the use of email marketing?

DR. MILLER: Yes, email is great. I have a newsletter that goes out about 1-3x/month. I actually think I could use it more effectively and am currently working on that.

CMT [Editor, Michael]: What creative methods have you used "inside" your practice to encourage positive word of mouth?

DR. MILLER: First, I try my hardest to make sure I continuously improve all my patients' health, make them feel great, and give them better customer service than I promised at sign-up. Second, I let them know that I am working hard on building my practice and treasure their referrals.

To connect with Dr. Shira Miller on Facebook, go to http://www.facebook.com/menopausedoctor.

"

The most effective tactics for businesses to reach customers through social media is with wall posts and direct messages.

"

Wi-Fi Is Now The Equivalent of Free Refills...It's Expected! So, make sure it's FREE and readily available in your practice.

When was the last time you went to a restaurant and they didn't refill your lemonade or water glass? Probably pretty rare. Well, free Wi-Fi is becoming the norm (as free refills are to the restaurant industry) in most modern medical practices. Hardly a quarter goes by without the news of skyrocketing smart phone sales and surging numbers involving mobile users accessing the Internet.

Smartphones offer distinct opportunities for your patients to "check-in" to your Facebook Page, (thus a referral to countless friends of that patient in just seconds...hello!). More and more practices are making it easier for patients to take advantage of these features by installing Wireless Routers in their practice. A wireless router can be purchased at any big-box retailer for under a $100. Free Wi-Fi is as simple and easy to implement in your practice and doesn't cost you any additional internet fees (in most areas). to your patients.

CHAPTER 10

YOU DON'T HAVE TO DO THIS ALONE.

There are plenty of resources available.

CHAPTER 10

YOU DON'T HAVE TO DO THIS ALONE.

There are plenty of resources available.

Concierge Medicine Today is pleased to announce that it has entered into a partnership with Social Blue Media. Social Blue helps physicians and their healthcare practices increase their online and offline business using the latest internet marketing strategies proven to get businesses page-one Google rankings and increased sales.

Social Blue works closely with Concierge Medicine Physicians to promote, persuade, and procure new patient leads into their practice using proven and strategic online marketing tools. The company offers an incredible array of services.

Learn more at: www.SocialBlueMedia.com

They [Social Blue Media] do not simply focus on basic internet marketing like most consultants, but they focus on helping to quickly grow your business by offering you.

- Internet Marketing Services

- Search Engine Optimization (SEO)

- Website Design

- Social Media

- Email Autoresponders

- Text Message Autoresponders

- Lead Generation Services

- And MUCH, MUCH More...

As stated before 72% of concierge physicians report that it takes more than three months to successfully sign a new patient into their practices. Over 90% of current concierge physicians still need more patients in order to close their practices at their desired patient thresholds. However, nearly 20% of concierge physicians fail in the first 24 months because of a lack of new patient leads and interest in their new business model. Also, the failure rate of physicians entering Concierge Medicine is growing. Just two years ago, it was less than 7%. Today, we've found that it's nearly 20%. We saw the need and searched for a quality company to help physicians build their practices. Countless concierge physicians throughout the U.S. can benefit significantly from the online marketing services Social Blue can provide."

As a result, *Concierge Medicine Today* is pleased to partner with Social Blue and its partners to help concierge physicians and businesses across America increase their online and offline business.

Social Media Management thru Social Blue Client Testimonials!

"They [Social Blue] are very passionate about their role and their results speak for themselves. You will find them to be very professional and detail oriented."

~ Timothy, Rural Pastor, Georgia

"Our web site traffic and store traffic have increased pretty dramatically since we started our online campaign. Traffic went up over 1,000%."

~ Little Rock, AR

To read more of Social Blue Testimonials from, visit: www.SocialBlueMedia.com

FREE WEBINAR
"How To Get 100 Customers In 100 Days!"

They want to challenge you to take them up on the "100 Patients in 100 Days" Challenge. They are hosting a **FREE webinar** that will show you 7 simple 'DotComSecrets' that will help you to get more patients almost instantly.

People have paid thousands of dollars to learn the SAME techniques that you will learn for **FREE** on this webinar - AND you'll be entered into our challenge to help YOU get at least 100 new patients in the next 100 days!

These strategies will increase your traffic and sales and they work in ANY economy! Reserve your FREE ticket to this groundbreaking webinar and change your business FOREVER! Simply visit www.SocialBlueMedia.com to proceed and save your spot today!

FREE 21-POINT MARKETING ANALYSIS – FREE!

For Concierge Medicine Today readers, Social Blue wants to challenge you to take them up on the "21-Point Marketing Analysis". They are offering to all Concierge Medicine Today physician readers a FREE 21-Point Marketing Analysis that will show you some simple steps that will help you to get more patients almost instantly. Business owners have paid thousands of dollars to learn the SAME techniques that you will learn for FREE in this analysis.

These strategies have increased traffic for many business owners and will increase your web and social media traffic and patient memberships. Reserve your FREE 21-POINT ANALYSIS with a Social Blue Representative today and change your practice FOREVER! Simply call (678) 597-2551, email info@socialbluemedia.com or visit: www.SocialBlueMedia.com.

FREE Local Business Visibility Report

Is your site visible to search engines? Is it getting traffic? To find out the answer right now just enter your phone number below to run your FREE visibility report.

Claim your free Online Visibility Report, visit: http://socialbluemedialocalsearchreport.visibilitysco re.com/ or visit www.SocialBlueMedia.com.

2-DISC AUDIO BOOK
Branding Concierge Medicine

Now available for your car, office or home, take

"Branding Concierge Medicine" with you anywhere.

Available now on a 2-disc audio book for only

$49.95 each.

Visit www.BrandingConciergeMedicine.com

Let me close by saying this. We are on this journey together and it's an honor to share this time with you. I trust you found this book or audio book helpful. It can change your business forever!

As I mentioned earlier, we've got a wealth of resources, news, education and information available at our web sites, www.AskTheCollective.org. Also, hop over to www.ConciergeMedicine101.com for helpful research and patient education material to use for free in your marketing.

Have a fantastic day and remember, visit us online for all the latest news, legal updates, insurance news and Concierge Medicine information at www.ConciergeMedicineToday.com.

SITED SOURCES & CREDITS

ConciergeMedicineToday.com

AskTheCollective.org

ConciergeMedicine101.com

SocialBlueMedia.com

MariSmith.com

Dotcomsecrets.com/your-value-ladder/

Facebook.com/menopausedoctor.

U.S. Bancorp's Piper Jaffray

Wired.com/business/2012/04/ff_spotfuture/all/.

CHAPTER 11

**ADDITIONAL ARTICLES about
CONCIERGE MEDICINE & helpful
RESOURCES**

Direct Primary Care and Concierge Medicine - What's the Difference?

By Michael Tetreault, Editor-In-Chief, Concierge Medicine Today
Published: November 9, 2009

The Difference Between Concierge Medicine and Direct Primary Care

Direct primary care (DPC) is a term often linked to its companion in health care, 'concierge medicine.' Although the two terms are similar and belong to the same family, concierge medicine is a term that fully embraces or 'includes' many different health care delivery models, direct primary care being one of them.

Similarities

DPC practices, similar in philosophy to their concierge medicine lineage - bypass insurance and go for a more 'direct' financial relationship with patients and also provide comprehensive care and preventive services for an affordable fee. However, DPC is only one branch in the family tree of concierge medicine.

DPC, like concierge health care practices, remove many of the financial barriers to 'accessing' care whenever care is needed. There are no insurance co-pays, deductibles or co-insurance fees. DPC practices also do not typically accept insurance payments, thus avoiding the overhead and complexity of maintaining relationships with insurers, which can consume as much as $0.40 of each medical dollar spent (See Sources Below).

Differences

According to sources (see below) DPC is a 'mass-market variant of concierge medicine, distinguished by its low prices.' Simply stated, the biggest difference between 'direct primary care' and retainer based practices is that DPC takes a low, flat rate fee whereas omodels, (although plans may vary by practice) - usually charge an annual retainer fee and promise more 'access' to the doctor.

According to *Concierge Medicine Today*, the first official news outlet for this marketplace, both health care delivery models are providing affordable, cost-effective health care to thousands of patients across the U.S. *Concierge Medicine Today* is also the only known organization that is officially tracking and collecting data on these practices and the physicians -- including the precise number of concierge physicians and practices throughout the U.S.

"This primary care business model [direct primary care] gives these type of providers the time to deliver more personalized care to their patients and pursue a comprehensive medical home approach," said Norm Wu, CEO of Qliance Medical Management based in Seattle, Washington. "One in which the provider's incentives are fully aligned with the patient's incentives."

References and Sources: *Direct Primary Care and Concierge Medicine - What's the Difference?*

- "Doc This Way!: Tech-Savvy Patients and Pros Work Up Healthcare 2.0". New York Post. 4/7/2009.
- Who Killed Marcus Welby? from Seattle's The Stranger, 1/23/2008
- "Direct Medical Practice - The Uninsured Solution to the Primary Medical Care Mess" with Dr. Garrison Bliss (Qliance Medical Group of WA).
- "Direct Primary Care: A New Brew In Seattle". Harvard Medical School - WebWeekly. 2008-03-03.
- DPCare.org
- Qliance.com
- ConciergeMedicineToday.com
- Concierge Medicine Today
  URL: http://www.ConciergeMedicineToday.com
  E: Editor@conciergemedicinetoday.com
- Article Source: http://EzineArticles.com/?expert=Michael_Tetreault
- Article Source: http://EzineArticles.com/3216545

Concierge Medicine Has A Story To Tell

By Michael Tetreault, Editor-In-Chief, Concierge Medicine Today
Published: March 22, 2010

A number of challenges face any physician looking to implement a concierge medicine or direct/private pay business model in their practice. In today's health care reform and rhetoric-rich society, we are witnessing the perfect storm of price transparency among doctors, a growing base of cost conscious patients and a lack of properly educated, consumer involvement.

It's a little known fact that over 90% of current concierge physicians need additional patients in order to reach their desired patient threshold. Numerous concierge physicians across the country need over 300 patients. Furthermore, preliminary results from a concierge medicine research poll over the past years has shown that nearly 20% of concierge physicians fail in the first 24 months due to a lack of participation in their new business model.

Let's face it, shifting a primary care practice that has been around for years into a retainer-based, relational practice or business model can be seen by many as elitist, bring up patient abandonment talk or by some as a welcome answer to a growing problem where patients actually say to their physician, 'thank you - I've been waiting for you to do this!'

There is no reason why patients, if properly and professionally educated, when shown the facts, cannot see the vast economical benefits and value through healthcare provided by a relationship-oriented and wellness-focused doctor. Concierge doctors offer something valuable and personally tailored to meet the needs of each of their patients. Each concierge physician should be congratulated for answering the call and providing quality care to their patients.

Before you find a concierge or membership medicine doctor near you will want to watch this video and find out the "3 Things Every Patient Needs To Know About Concierge Medicine" at [http://www.conciergemedicinetoday.com]

There is also a valuable, educational resource now available for patients seeking such care at www.conciergemedicine101.com.

Article Source: http://EzineArticles.com/3807234

Concierge Medicine –
Deal Or No Deal?

By *Michael Tetreault, Editor-In-Chief, Concierge Medicine Today*
Published: April 22, 2010

If there's one thing I've learned in the past several years about concierge medicine and researching this emerging health care market, it's that people really don't understand it's not about price. I like to think of those pioneering doctors of the past who carry around a medical bag with a stethoscope inside and who come to the aid of my family and our bedside as visionary physicians who wanted to "normalize" their practice and get back to practicing medicine before 1950.

So, here are the top six (6) items every patient should truly understand about concierge medicine:

1) AVAILABILITY

Yes! It really is possible for a doctor to provide 24/7 access to his/her patients... and no -- this is not just some marketing tactic that seeks to over promise and under deliver. There's now evidence that when a doctor reduces his/her practice from its original size of 2,000 - 5,000 patients down to 300 - 600, he or she is choosing to "normalize" their practice and provide more availability and access to each patient. Inturn, that patient gets to really know the doctor and there is a bond and friendship that is formed.

2) COST

It doesn't cost a lot... it actually costs less than my cell phone bill. Over 50% of current concierge medicine fees cost an average or $1,500 per year or less than $135 per month. (Source 1) The USANetwork's breakout hit Royal Pains is entertaining -- the overwhelming majority is that most concierge medicine or private medical plans cater to those who can't afford the high health insurance premiums their used to paying with large health plan carriers.

3) CELL PHONE ACCESS

YES! They actually do pick up the phone and it's not a nurse or staff person. If you are enrolled in a concierge medical practice, then you are paying an annual or monthly fee for "enhanced access" and a close relationship with your physician. That's right, the unthinkable has become a true reality. Doctors are now giving their cell phone numbers to their patients and they are the ones picking up the calls.

4) SAME DAY APPOINTMENTS

Included in most membership medicine fees is same day appointments and enhanced access to you doctor. In fact, a recent poll conducted by the Collective found that 100% of concierge physicians promise and actually deliver "same day" appointments.

5) WHAT I REALLY NEED WILL BE INCLUDED

It's a well known fact that approximately 88% of the average persons health care can be handled by their primary care or family physician. Thus, concierge medicine services typically offered inside these plans usually include: physical exams, blood work, unlimited office visits and other services. These annual or monthly fees typically cover basic services that include preventive care, routine physicals, longer appointments, next-day appointments, 24-hour-a-day phone access and e-mail, house calls, coordination of care when you travel, and an interactive medical ID bracelet in case of an emergency.

6) IS IT COMPATIBLE WITH MY INSURANCE?

A recent study was conducted (Source 2) with this question in mind. The result of the study found that most concierge medicine physicians (nearly 80%) practice inside a business model called a "Hybrid" practice. Hybrid meaning these doctors accept most insurance plans along with offering the delivery or 24/7 cell phone access to your doctor, no wait appointments, call-in prescriptions and more via a monthly or annual retainer.

Before you find a concierge or membership medicine doctor near you will want to watch this video and find out the "3 Things Every Patient Needs To Know About Concierge Medicine" at www.ConciergeMedicineToday.com.

There is also a valuable, educational resource now available for patients seeking such care at http://www.ConciergeMedicineToday.com.

Sources and Resources

- Concierge Medicine Today
- The Concierge Medicine Research Collective
- Article Source: http://EzineArticles.com/?expert=Michael_Tetreault
- Article Source: http://EzineArticles.com/4079755

Concierge Medicine - Shedding (Not Shifting) Costs

By *Michael Tetreault, Editor-In-Chief, Concierge Medicine Today*
Published: May 4, 2010

Concierge medicine has long been thought to be too expensive and only serves the rich and affluent. This article will debunk this myth that has been around for years. According to recent polls among concierge medical physicians from across the U.S., these polls have revealed that more than 50% of current concierge medicine fees cost less than $135 per month and on average, $1,500 per year. (Source 1). Another surprising finding by the same source is that "price" is not first on the list when patients seek the care of such physicians.

A recent survey asked private medical physician what is the most common type of question that you encounter when patients want to inquire about your type of practice model or join your practice. The answers were surprising to many and they are listed (in order of importance to patients): insurance compatibility; Medicare acceptance; and price.

IS IT COMPATIBLE WITH MY INSURANCE?

Another survey among this type of physician practice (Source 2) with insurance compatibility in mind found that most concierge medicine physicians, nearly 80%, work or practice inside a medical practice or business model called a "Hybrid" practice. Hybrid meaning these doctors accept most insurance plans along with offering the delivery or 24/7 cell phone access to your doctor, no wait appointments, call-in prescriptions and much more. They in turn charge each patient a monthly or annual fee for these enhanced services.

Because the overwhelming majority of concierge medicine or private medical plans cater to those who cannot afford the high health insurance premiums, these types of medical practices across America can and should now be seen as one of the most affordable options for patients who are used to paying large health plan premiums.

And when you are ready to find a concierge doctor near you or learn more about the benefits and cost of joining a concierge medical practice, there is a valuable, educational resource now available for patients seeking such care at http://www.ConciergeMedicineToday.com.

Author and Sources

- Michael Tetreault, Concierge Medicine Today
- http://www.askthecollective.org.
- Author: Michael Tetrault, Editor-In-Chief, Concierge Medicine Today
- To learn more about concierge medicine and to find a physician or doctor near you, please visit http://www.ConciergeMedicineToday.com.

- Article Source: http://EzineArticles.com/?expert=Michael_Tetreault
- Article Source: http://EzineArticles.com/4158233

Concierge Doctors, Stop "Chasing" Patients

By *Michael Tetreault, Editor-In-Chief, Concierge Medicine Today*
Published: August 3, 2010

There is nothing more frustrating than spending a few thousand dollars on a postcard or letter and a week later your office received five phone calls, one email and 43 return to sender stickers.

This form of marketing is what advertising agencies call "push" marketing. This form of marketing "pushes" a product or service onto an individual when they are not yet ready to buy or learn more about your service. The goal of such campaigns is to create TOMA or Top of Mind Awareness.

The Problem With "Push" Marketing. It's expensive and the ROI (return on investment) is minimal.

The Solution. "Pull" Marketing.

"Pull" Marketing is a marketing approach that allows you to gradually attract prospective patients to your business when they are ready. With the advent of internet marketing, Google and Social Media, "Pull" marketing has been proven to be successful in tracking ROI, dollars spent, clicks, hits, and much, much more.

Since every doctor and their office staff are constantly looking for that one unique golden nugget of marketing wisdom, today I'll tell you what NOT to do when advertising your practice in PRINT.

The biggest mistake people make when promoting a product, person or program in print is...they don't include a low-risk offer.

Bottom Line - If you are currently using "Push" marketing and would like to learn more about the benefits and cost-effectiveness of "Pull" marketing in helping to grow your concierge medicine practice, you will want to connect with a social media marketing agency that understands these core principles.

If you liked this post and would like to learn more about concierge medicine, you should visit a great resource for concierge doctors and their patients called Concierge Medicine Today http://www.conciergemedicinetoday.com.

Article Source: http://EzineArticles.com/?expert=Michael_Tetreault

Article Source: http://EzineArticles.com/4749339

4 Mistakes to Avoid When Selecting Your Next Primary Care Or Family Doctor

By Michael Tetreault, Editor-In-Chief, Concierge Medicine Today
Published: August 16, 2010

1) Is Eight Minutes Enough Time For Your Doctor To Collect 25 Years of Family History?

Most doctors are busy and they have huge waiting rooms full of people that they need to treat. If you visit your doctor for an average of 8 minutes per visit and schedule a visit 6 times per year, you've spent less than 60 minutes with your doctor throughout an entire year! Is that really enough time for your doctor to get to know you and make a good assessment of your health risks based on your current condition and family history?

2) Does your doctor have to look at your chart to remember your name?

'Nuff said. I think you get the point here.

3) How full is the waiting room?

Just because the waiting room and parking lot is full, doesn't mean you've found the best doctor. In today's day and age of insurance, doctors join hundreds of insurance plans in order to get their practice listed in more directories. The more directories that the doctor is listed in, the more likely that his/her practice is going to be full of patients that know nothing about him. As you are probably aware, these directories tell you nothing about the doctor, his medical background, patient testimonials, wait-time, etc.

4) Does your doctor's office have two waiting rooms?

The answer you are looking for here us either two (2) or none. Just a few days ago, I visited my dermatologists office. He separated his practice as soon as I walked in by asking patient to go right or left. Right was for 'cash only' patients and the left was for 'Insurance Patients'.

Do you want to know the difference between the 'Cash Only' waiting room and the 'Insurance' side? Let me tell you, there was a big difference. As a cash paying patient, the waiting room was turned into a lobby, there were refreshments, fresh coffee, cold juice, a flat screen tv playing the latest news and more. People were happy.

On the insurance side, there were frowns, ugly furniture, old paint and nine people waiting.

The next time I'm looking for a doctor, I'm not going to look in a directory. I'm going to look for a color photo, a well-written profile, some details about the doctor I'm seeing, hopefully find some positive and refreshing patient testimonials and have the attitude of anticipation and excitement. If you'd like to find a great doctor who will spend more time with you and reward you with a positive patient experience the next time you visit their office, watch this video at www.conciergemedicinetoday.com.

Article Source:

http://EzineArticles.com/?expert=Michael_Tetreault

Article Source: http://EzineArticles.com/4836275

Concierge Medicine Doctors - Patients Retention Higher Than Others

By *Michael Tetreault, Editor-In-Chief, Concierge Medicine Today*
Published: September 15, 2010

According to 2010 poll results conducted among retainer-based and boutique physicians from across the U.S. in May of 2010, findings indicate that 60% of these types of physicians retain their members for roughly 7 to 9 years and longer. These polls have also found that the national retention average for a traditional physician (i.e primary care, family practice, internist, etc.) participating with multiple insurance companies, managed care, etc., retained their people for about 5 to 7 years. I believe this number will only increase as people find out how affordable and relational these types of practices and doctors really are.

It's unfortunate that somewhere between the late 1950's and the year 2010, the connection between the doctor and his or her patient was lost. Long gone are the days where our doctor carries a medical bag and visits my house. When medicine became regulated by the government that relationship was quickly eroded and eventually extinguished from our home and our memory. It's not to say that some form of administration needed to be formulated back then, but now administrative tasks and regulation tasks take up most of the time of our doctors that they must look at a chart or a file to know our name.

In my conversations and surveys with numerous boutique, retainer and direct primary care physicians from across the country, these doctors offices needed to complete eight pages of paper work for one patient to receive a $4 prescription. In this new business model of primary care and family medicine popping up across the U.S., hundreds of doctors have learned that there is a better way.

Why will it grow?

Relationship! Relationship! Relationship! This movement in medicine is based on relationship. When I have a doctor that I know I can call day or night and that he will actually pick up the phone, that's priceless...and that's true relationship.

Because this movement is relatively young and data to support the exact number people at any given concierge medical practice for longer than 10-15 years is limited. However, I believe that as we continue to track in the years ahead and follow retention data of these practices that we will learn just how happy so many people are with these types of old-fashioned health care delivery model offices verses a traditional primary care practice.

Soon, we'll find the "happiness" and "healthy" gap between them to be much greater.

Figuratively, this longer-lasting and more personal relationship will result in greater retention data and further solidify concierge medicine's rightful place in the healthcare market. These types of doctors emphasize that what's important to people is true relationship with their doctor and actual dollar-cost savings each month and every year. These are key findings and critical factors in the renewals of membership medicine or direct primary care plans from across the country. I'm very glad to know that there are no a lot of doctors working smarter, not harder and are keeping people coming back year after year. Indeed, there is renewable energy to be found in this form of medicine.

The Concierge Medicine Research Collective serves as an educational resource on all things concierge medicine. To learn more about this topic and emerging healthcare delivery model among primary care and family care physicians, you might want to visit: http://www.AskTheCollective.org or http://www.ConciergeMedicineToday.com.

Article Source: http://EzineArticles.com/?expert=Michael_Tetreault

Article Source: http://EzineArticles.com/4414152

Medical Homes - Where Everyone Is Invited, Is Included, Is Important

By Michael Tetreault, Editor-In-Chief, Concierge Medicine Today
Published: January 25, 2011

When was the last time your doctor inspired you to do the right thing for your health, yourself or the health of your family? I can tell you from one of own recent experiences that inspiration isn't starting inside the waiting room of my PCP or on the phone disputing a claim with customer no-service and trying to talk to some big insurance company.

In the new world of medicine, medical homes and concierge medicine are delivering some big results. These health care providers and the businesses they operate are successful in today's difficult marketplace because of timing, technology, relationship and the listening ear you receive from every physician you meet inside these practices.

So, what exactly is making medical homes (sometimes referred to as concierge care or concierge medicine) attractive, affordable and inviting to everyone? It's summed up in five words. Price. Compatibility. Relationship. Technology. Accessibility.

Medical Homes Are: Affordable.

Concierge medical care and direct pay medical business models are on the forefront of modern business and innovation. Like Taco Bell, the originator of the 'value menu,' many modern medical practices across America are actually starting to list their prices to their patients before they buy.

Until recently, primary care and health care practices were one of the only businesses in America that rarely listed how much they charged for services and products. The eventual evolution of retainer based health care, direct primary care and concierge medical business models changed all of that. Then along came the recession in 2008 that changed the world as we know it. People started paying more attention to their credit card statements, health insurance claims, hospital bills and prescription drug costs.

An independent analysis of concierge medicine and direct pay primary care practices across the U.S. have shown that nearly 60% of physicians using this form of price transparency are costing patients less than $136 per month. Compare that to the insurance premiums of large health plan carriers and the savings are monumental. This is just one of the new ways to inspire hope in difficult economic times.

"People want 'the deal,'" says one concierge physician. "We, the doctors, must be the first one to the market to be honest with their customer...we need to take the first step. For too long we've waited. Decades in-fact, for insurance companies and managed care organizations to provide some form of user-friendly price transparency. It just hasn't happened. It's simply become to complicated, until now."

Medical Homes Are: Compatible.

An independent study analyzing concierge medical and direct pay health care practices across America for the past three years reports that 80% of these types of practices and physicians accept insurance. Sound like a contradiction? I thought the whole purpose of price transparency and direct pay health care was to do away with insurance complexities?

So, why are so many of these practices across America (80% in fact) allowing their patients to use their insurance too? Because insurance is still important to most people. You see, the physicians and business executives who operate these types of modern medical practices understand that you cannot take away the freedom of people's choice to use their insurance, when necessary.

Despite the enormous complexity and erroneous amounts of work these insurance plans carry with them, it's still every patients right to carry and use their health insurance beyond the retainer of fee they pay for comprehensive service from their physician.

"Patients continue to carry their insurance because of hospitalization or emergency room visits," says one Texas family physician. "We encourage them to call us first if they have an allergic reaction or other severe health issue but if they need to go to the hospital, that type of service can't be paid for inside our financial relationship with the patient. So, having that backup plan in your wallet or purse is more useful than you might think."

Say what you will, but the next time you feel compelled to pay cash to your doctor go for it. They'll appreciate it and you might even be saving a tree or two with all of the paperwork you've saved. If you'd like to find a medical home, concierge physician or direct pay physician in your area or simply learn more about them, you will want to visit http://www.ConciergeMedicineToday.com.

Article Source: http://EzineArticles.com/?expert=Michael_Tetreault

Article Source: http://EzineArticles.com/5749109

Concierge Medicine - The Cure for Bad Moods

By Michael Tetreault, Editor-In-Chief, Concierge Medicine Today
Published: January 25, 2011

Do you or your kids suffer from bad moods when you leave the doctor's office? Does having a doctor's appointment effect your mood for the entire day when you know you're going to have to take time off of work or get a sitter for the kids just to be left waiting in a waiting area with old magazines? Well, your not alone but you're in luck because there is a cure.

In the mid 1990's a new form of primary and family medicine was reinvented to work in today's busy health care marketplace. It's called concierge medical care or direct pay health care. It's actually really simple. If you want to see the doctor, you call him and he or she actually pick up the phone. You tell them what you need and determine the urgency of the situation and most often, you're seen in as little amount of time as it takes you to get to their office. Sometimes, the doctor will even come to your home, your office or schedule a time to video chat with you over a secure internet connection.

How Do I Pay The Doctor?

This is the amazing part. These visioneering physicians accept cash and many times, will tell you how much their service costs before you buy anything. Simple, right? Up until just the past few years, the health care marketplace was the only industry in America where consumers of service (ie patients) had no idea how much things cost. And, a survey summary released in July of 2010 reports that nearly 60 percent of these types of physicians cost as little as $136 per month.

What About Insurance?

Most physicians operating within this new way of doing business in their medical practice accept insurance. Eighty percent actually according to independent studies released in 2010.

If you have health insurance, your concierge doctor may submit claims for treatments that are not covered under your membership.

What Services Are Included In The Annual Retainer Fee?

A lot of these physicians have common services they offer to their patients throughout the year that are included in one low annual fee, payable in the form of monthly, quarterly or semi-annual payments. Those services typically offered are: comprehensive physical exams, routine blood work, unlimited visits to the office, same or next day appointments, phone-in prescription renewals requests, casts, routine vaccines, 24-hour-a-day phone access and e-mail, house calls, coordination of care when you travel, immediate family counsel for those family members visiting you and much, much more.

What If I Need To Go To The Hospital or Emergency Room?

Independent polls among concierge physicians across the U.S. show that over 90% of concierge medical physicians help patients navigate through the emergency room faster and more efficiently because the admitting physician (ie their very own concierge doctor) had hospital privileges and not only that, knew that patients exact medical history, current prescription usage and more.

As it relates to insurance, patients of concierge medical programs are encouraged to maintain their insurance for hospitalization or emergency room visits. Those type of services are not included in annual fees paid to a concierge physician.

Find a concierge physician near you and heed this advice and you, your family and everyone around you just might be happier! There is a helpful web site I recommend along with videos, news and research that

will help you find a physician near you. Visit
http://www.ConciergeMedicineToday.com.

Article Source:

http://EzineArticles.com/?expert=Michael_Tetreault

Article Source: http://EzineArticles.com/5749998

Value Menu Medicine Is Here

By *Michael Tetreault, Editor-In-Chief, Concierge Medicine Today*
Published: January 27, 2011

Like one very large Mexican fast food chain and the
creator of the 'value menu' concept, a lot of modern
health care business centers and physicians from across
the U.S. are now actually starting to show their prices to
their customers (ie patients) before they see the doctor.
Up until recently, primary care and health care practices
were one of the only segments in the U.S. that rarely
listed how much their fees were for their time, services
and products.

The recent evolution of retainer based health care,
concierge medical business models and direct primary
care practices changed all of that. Concierge medical
practices are becoming widely popular among a diverse
population of people.

However, there is a population of people, mainly those
in the media, who understand these types of medical
models offered by visioneering physicians across
America (and now growing across the globe) to be
exclusive, elusive and let's say it, flat out wrong.

Having spoken to physicians, interviewed experts and
been interviewed myself in the past many years, I've
found that there is real data now available to the public

that shows this type of medical care to be exceptionally high quality and affordable. In fact, I've found this dynamic and ever evolving industry to be an all-inclusive, inviting and a win-win for anyone looking for something different from their doctor.

Why Is A Concierge Medical Practice A Win-Win For Patients & Family?

• Decreasing Hospitalizations:

A third-party evaluation of recent data shows that concierge medical patients had over 61 percent fewer hospitalizations when compared with similar patients in commercial insurance plans. Not to mention, 74 percent fewer hospitalizations when compared with Medicare patients of similar gender, age, and disease risk.

Plain and simple, concierge medical patients hospital utilization rates are lower, even when you try matching demographic variables from one age to another. In 2006, many concierge practices had a total average hospitalization rate of less than 120 admissions per one thousand admissions. In non-concierge medical practices, the rate was over 226 per one thousand admissions. On average, a huge population of concierge medical patients had 107 fewer admissions per one thousand than people in standard insurance plans. It's appropriate to say 'wow' at this point. That's a 47 percent reduction in hospitalizations.

• Concierge Medical Care Prevents and Prevents and Prevents. Here's Proof:

Data when studying concierge medical practices over the past few years has shown that preventable hospitalizations are lowered by 40% in concierge medical practices. In fact, one source shows that avoidable hospitalization rates average less than 17 admissions per one thousand people. In standard health insurance plans with completely comparable patient populations, the rate is over 28 admits per one thousand patients.

All We See And Hear In The Media Is That All Concierge Medical Practices Are Exclusive And Really, Really...Expensive. Come on...Really?

• Hard Data Analyzed Over Years Shows Almost 60% of Concierge Medical Programs Cost Less Than $136 per month.

This should be a wake up call for all of those critics and cynics in the marketplace thinking this is high-priced, luxury medical care for the rich. Utilizing a blended rate based upon national averages for current fees charged for concierge medical care, an estimated 9,285,714,286 people could be provided concierge medical care with the 13 trillion dollar debt. Carrying this out 928,571,429 people could be provided this care for 10 years.*

So If It's So Affordable, That Means I Won't Get Much...Right? Wrong.

Independent analyses show clearly that concierge-models deliver superior clinical outcomes compared to conventional insurance-based practices. Dr. Lee, a practicing concierge physician based in Florida indicates that when you have time to deal with the issues, you do better.

Services typically offered by most concierge medical physicians include: physical exams, blood work, unlimited office visits and other services (see many of the most common services listed below).

Membership fees typically cover basic services that include preventive care, routine physicals, longer appointments, next-day appointments, 24-hour-a-day phone access and e-mail, house calls, coordination of care when you travel, and a CD with your medical records. If you have health insurance, your concierge doctor may submit claims for treatments that are not covered under your membership. Some of the most common services include: On call 24/7 access; House calls; No waiting; Unlimited appointments for your membership fee; "Executive physical exams" that include a full body scan, screening for over 180 diseases, blood tests for rare conditions and time spent with a physician going over every aspect of your medical history. These comprehensive exams can cost well into the thousands through traditional channels; Lab tests; X-rays; Coordination of care if you become ill while traveling; Mental health services; Well-baby checks; Acute care visits; Online access to medical records; Home delivery of medications; Hospital visits from the doctor; Transportation to appointments; Coordinated care with specialists during travel; Hotel reservations for family during a medical crisis; Wellness, fitness and lifestyle screenings; Weight management; Nutritional counseling; and more.

Concierge Care, Direct Pay and Retainer Based Physician-Patient Practices Are 'Relationship-Oriented and Experience-Rich'

The more doctors (not office managers, staff or nurses), communicate with patients face-to-face and provide other value-driven options, the more those patients will come back again and again and better yet, tell their friends and family to see you too.

What primary care of family medical practice do you know of today that spends more than forty five to ninety minutes with each patient on every visit? If you would like to read more about these types of physicians or find a doctor near you, you may want to watch this video that talks more in detail about concierge care, retainer or direct pay physicians at http://www.ConciergeMedicineToday.com.

IMPORTANT NOTE: Each patient should check with their physician to find out what services are included in their individual membership. These are only examples of some of the services. Your physician practice and membership may or may not include some or all of these types of services.

*The figures shown and facts shown here have been analyzed, published and collected internally by information and resources obtained and conducted by Concierge Medicine Today.

Article Source: http://EzineArticles.com/?expert=Michael_Tetreault

Article Source: http://EzineArticles.com/5741117

The 20 Minute Rule of Social Media Engagement: Morning, Noon and Night.

By Michael Tetreault, Editor-In-Chief, Concierge Medicine Today
Published: January 6, 2012

I recently learned that one of the greatest software and computer developers said early on in his career (and I'm paraphrasing), that the person who creates 'online communities' over the Internet will make millions.

While this computer designer missed his opportunity to create one of the largest online communities in the world, how true does that statement ring with us today? Our entire online world is all about community these days isn't it?

According to a recent infographic I saw recently each Facebook user spends on average 15 hours and 33 minutes a month on the site. As a marketing professional whose job it is to spend time and money on these sites, I certainly enjoy these online communities and lose track of time -- until I started applying a personal sixty-minute rule to my daily marketing activities.

Yes, it's true. I am the first to agree that it's hard to escape the allure of looking up old friends on Facebook, watching the latest movie trailer on YouTube, RT-ing on

Twitter, Digg-'n stuff and Meeting Up with like-minded colleagues on MeetUp. These addictive, enticing and tempting platforms must not distract us from our purpose which is to engage our fans and followers and be "social" in a way that spurs conversation and dialogue with those people who know, like and trust us and our business.

It's no secret that social media is a disruptive force in marketing for business professionals in this modern day of technological innovation and relationally-challenged age. Social media has changed the world of marketing for years to come. Just imagine if the printing press, radio, television, the brochure, the business card, newspapers and bill boards were all invented and released to the public all at the same time. That would be a lot for any one business to capture effectively. Essentially, that significant learning curve and workload was released to marketers and businesses because of social media just in the past few years.

But after spending hundreds (if not thousands) of hours inside the time sucking bubble of these alluring socially-centered sites, I can tell you it is absolutely possible to manage and navigate your entire business and marketing presence in sixty minutes a day.

I'm convinced that those who learn to manage their time better and be more productive will be the marketeers in social media marketing that will excel to the level of experts in their profession. Yes, Marketeers like myself spend enormous amounts of time managing our online presence -- but that's our job. We're supposed to be online updating our various Pages, Channels and Twitter feeds. Now, with the advent of social media dashboards or online command centers my daily logins and work in social media has changed dramatically in the past few years.

Here are some helpful tips and resources I use on a regular basis.

Create Your Profiles and Then Start Controlling and Managing Your Profiles.

Once your profiles are designed, updated with the appropriate marketing detail, and you become experienced with engaging, posting, and sharing content on each of the platforms you've chosen that are most pertinent to your business and target audience, you can do social media in 60 minutes a day.

Why Are Social Media Dashboards Important?

- Dashboards allow you to manage multiple social profiles
- Dashboards allow you to track your brand mentions

- Dashboards allow you to analyze social media fans, followers and obtain detailed traffic analyses
- Dashboards allow you to see the bulk of your profiles on one screen
- Dashboards allow you to schedule posts days, weeks and months in advance across multiple social media profiles and sites.
- Dashboards allow you to engage from one place as opposed to several individual platforms.

If you don't currently use a dashboard for the majority of your activity, it will absolutely change your perspective on and engagement in social media. Dashboards eliminate the need to log into several social media platforms and you can stop toggling between screens -- all of which will be a big time-saver. Trust me, I'm speaking from experience here.

Explore Your Options and Choose The Right Dashboard That Works For You.

There's plenty of options to choose from. You can choose Hootsuite, TweetDeck, Sprout Social, Ping.fm, NetVibes, MarketMeSuite, Jungle Torch, Trackur and more. There's too many to list, but explore some of them. Most have free accounts or trial periods that allow you to really choose the one that works best for you.

The 20 Minute Rule of Social Media Engagement: Morning, Noon and Night.

Whether you use your dashboard to engage with your fans or followers, following one simple rule will allow you to effectively "be social" in sixty minutes a day. When you commit twenty minutes in the morning, twenty minutes mid-day and twenty minutes in the early evening or before the 5-o'clock bell, there is enough time to greet your followers/fans; post updates to your profiles; post some (not all) of your original content; re-post your content; engage with people across your platforms; respond and reply to questions/mentions, and maintain a visibly, active business and personal profile online. Using this "Be Social In Sixty Minutes A Day" will now give you enough time to keep your profiles relevant, current, educational, social and visible on a daily basis.

And remember, social media is about having a conversation with those who know, like and trust you online. It's not a megaphone for your businesses. If you're curious about how to use social media dashboards or how to grow your business online using social media, watch our FREE webinar, "How To Get 100 Customers In 100 Days," just visit http://www.SocialBlueMedia.com.

Article Source:
http://EzineArticles.com/?expert=Michael_Tetreault

Article Source: http://EzineArticles.com/6772341

Why do patients leave their concierge physician?

By Michael Tetreault, Editor-In-Chief, Concierge Medicine Today
Published: April 25, 2012

As many people are aware, this type of boutique medicine or direct relationship medical practice delivery model concept is still relatively new. The greatest amount of data compiled to date on the loyalty or renewal rates of concierge medicine patients year after year tells us that these practices have an annual renewal rate of about 90.%. Additionally, these types of practices are mainly considered Hybrid business models, which means these doctors and their offices accept insurance and charge an annual retainer fee to their patients for enhanced access. This number is based on data from approximately 100,000 patients nationally.

Retention figures inside concierge medical care practices have proven consistent since the year 2000 but Concierge Medicine Today sources have informed us that these retention numbers are slowly declining due to one major factor -- some doctors are over-promising and under-delivering. This inturn, leaves the patient unsatisfied. On the positive side, these patients leaving their concierge care physician are overwhelmingly still choosing concierge-style medical care -- albeit just from a another physician in their geographic area.

Long term data on these particular kinds of patients is currently still being compiled but our data supporting the cost effectiveness and affordability of these healthcare models is intriguing. According to various physician journals, a patient will remain a patient of a traditional primary care doctor in a typical family practice or general medicine practice, barring an altering event (like a geographic move, death, loss of job, or other unforeseen circumstance) for 5-7 years.

Based upon the data listed above, it appears that retainer medicine or boutique physicians that have a long, relational-history with their patients are reporting higher retention levels that exceed traditional primary care and family practice expectations. This data combined with the fact that this model of medicine provides for closer communication and relationship with people -- we expect that the majority of patients will continue to remain with a retainer-based practitioner even longer than seven (7) years.

The information provided here gives more evidence that these types of medical practices are not just for the deep-pocketed executive. In fact, we have recently learned that over 50% of these types of healthcare consumers make a combined household income of less than $100,000 per year.

All of this data should be very encouraging to the public, as well as the practicing physician anywhere in America. This concept, initially thought of by many as healthcare for the rich -- is now accessible and very affordable for couples, seniors on Medicare, young families and individuals.

To learn more about the benefits and services concierge physicians provide to their patients, go to Concierge Medicine Today's patient education and resource center at www.ConciergeMedicine101.com.

ABOUT THE AUTHOR

Michael Tetreault

Senior Director of Online Services

 Michael C. Tetreault serves as the Editor-In-Chief of Concierge Medicine Today and the Executive Director of The Concierge Medicine Research Collective. He brings over 14 years of experience as a marketing, public relations, sales and brand manager. Mr. Tetreault also serves as the Senior Director of Online Services for Social Blue Media. As Senior Director of Online Services at Social Blue Media, Mr. Tetreault oversees all online aspects of advertising, public relations, events, new business R&D and reputation management activities

Mr. Tetreault's marketing and business development efforts have been featured in: *Town and Country Magazine; Fox Business Network; Fox Sports Net; Reuters; Gannett; The Chicago Tribune; Bloomberg News; The American General* and other prominent publications. Mr. Tetreault's previous experience includes serving as a public relations and fundraising consultant to non-profit organizations in which he provided marketing advice and fundraising expertise to their causes.

He was also responsible for coordinating their community partnerships, charitable events, marketing materials, web-site development and media relations.

He is considered an expert in the field of concierge medicine, an innovator in the marketplace of concierge medical care and an evangelist for the education of concierge medicine across the U.S. Additionally, labeled by *EzineArticles*, an Expert Author, authoring such works as "Social Media Marketing In Sixty Minutes A Day," "Branding Concierge Medicine" and many more.

Among Mr. Tetreault's accomplishments is the creation of two community health care and volunteer programs, *The Go Fish Project* and *Healthy Town USA. The Go Fish Project* is a benevolence program in which health care providers donate time, money and services to designated charities each year. *Healthy Town USA*, is an event management program that provides opportunity for health care professionals to volunteer and inturn connects them with world-class professional athletes. Under Mr. Tetreault's direction, these initiatives have developed marketing partnerships with: *AARP; ADP; Dannon Yogurt; Habitat For Humanity; The United Way; Kaiser Permanente Health Plans; USAA Duathlon*

World and National Championships; ITU Duathlon World and National Championships; USA Triathlon; *the Marine Corps Marathon* and many others. Mr. Tetreault was the first public relations strategist to incorporate chiropractic health care services into the Marine Corps Marathon in 2003.

Mr. Tetreault continues to serve as a strategic marketing and public relations consultant for many professional organizations. Mr. Tetreault is a graduate of The Fund Raising School Program from the Center on Philanthropy at Indiana University Purdue University Indianapolis, and a graduate of the Marketplace Alliance Entrepreneurial Development Program based in Atlanta, Georgia. Mr. Tetreault graduated Cum Laude from Lee University in Tennessee where he received two Bachelor of Arts (B.A.) degrees, Marketing/Advertising and Public Relations/Journalism. Mr. Tetreault is the recipient of the Inbound Marketing Certificate of Excellence by Inbound Marketing University [less than 2,000 across the U.S. have received this distinction] and is also a Certified Independent Marketing Advisor with DotComSecrets Local.

BRANDING
CONCIERGE
MEDICINE

**The Blueprint That Shows You How To Apply
The Foundational Principles of Effective
Marketing
To Grow Your Medical Practice.**

Author: Michael Tetreault

Publisher Elite MD, Inc.
4080 McGinnis Ferry Road
Building 800, Suite 801
Alpharetta, Georgia 30005

Romans 15:13

I pray that God, who gives hope, will bless you with complete happiness and peace because of your faith. And may the power of the Holy Spirit fill you with hope.

Contemporary English Version (CEV)

Made in the USA
Charleston, SC
18 July 2014